Vol 9

MAZE

FOR KIDS

Ages 4-6

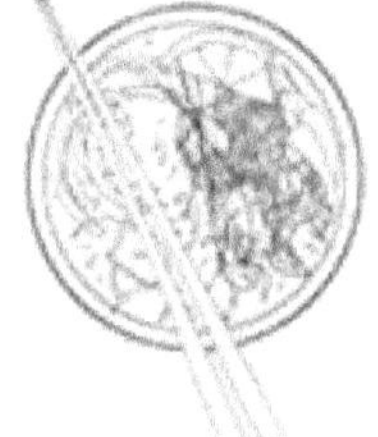

MAZE BOOK

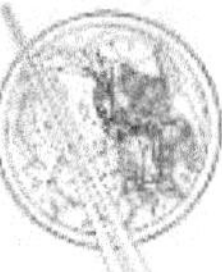

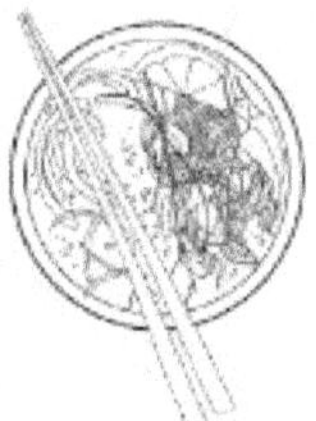

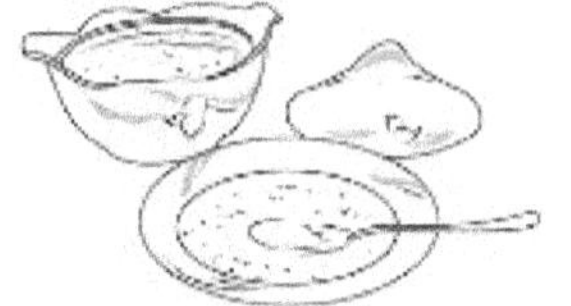

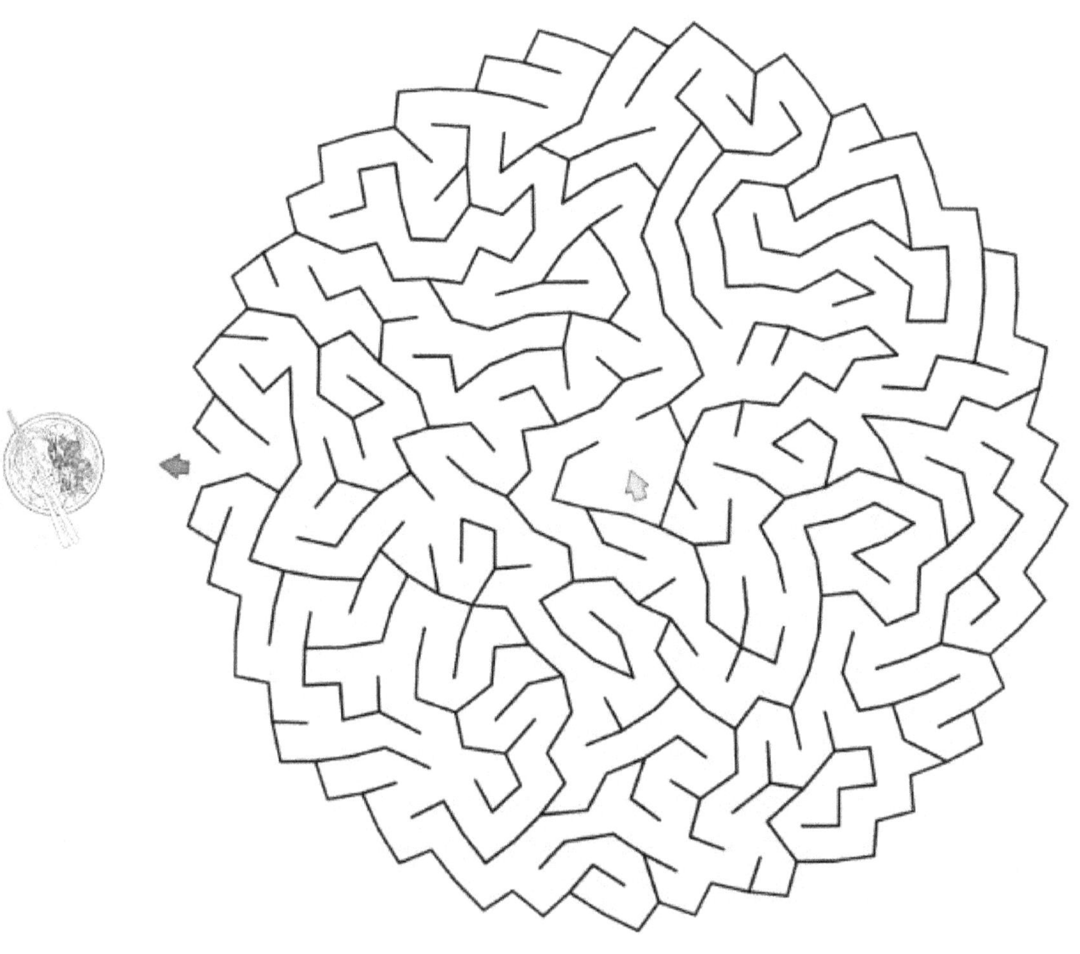

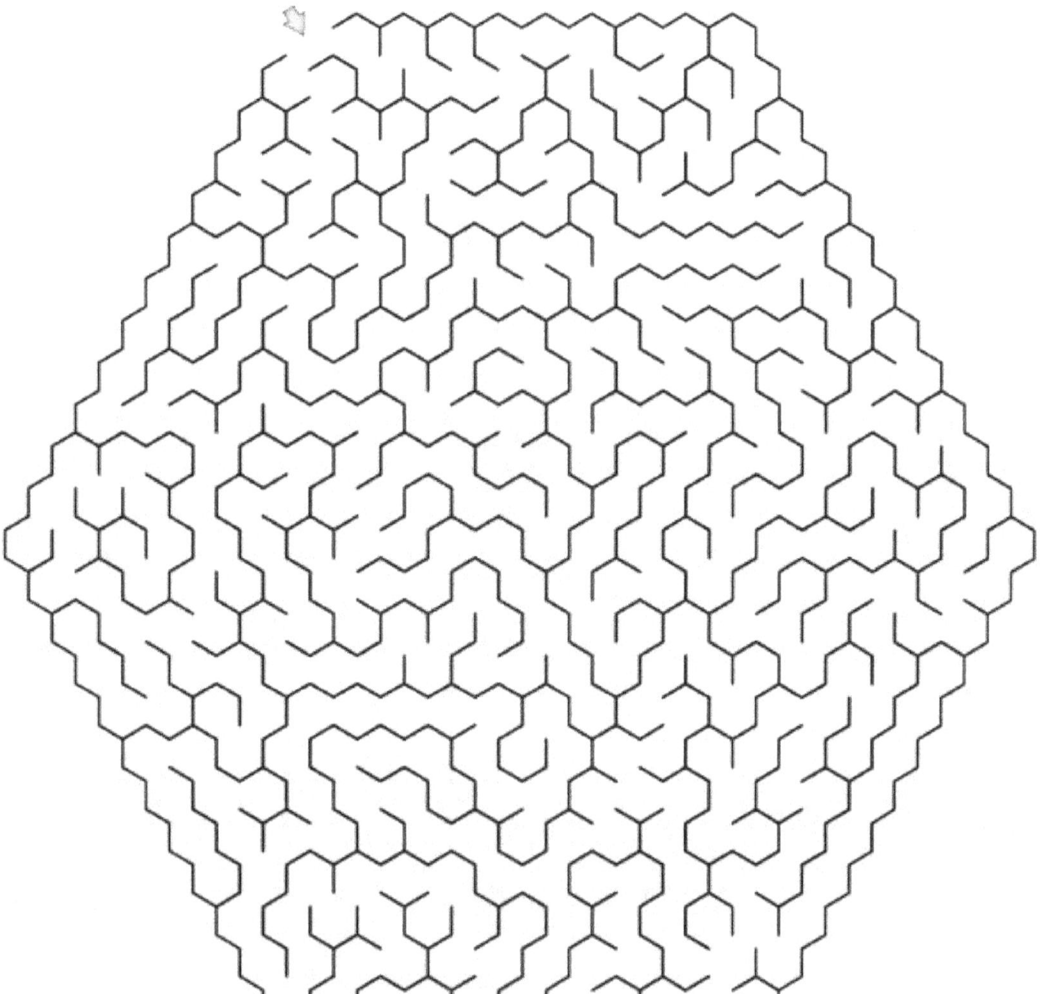

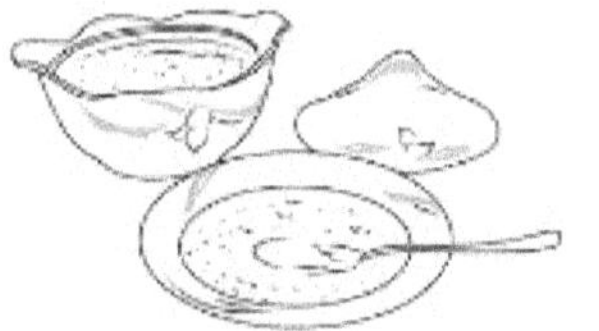

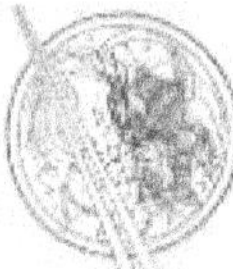

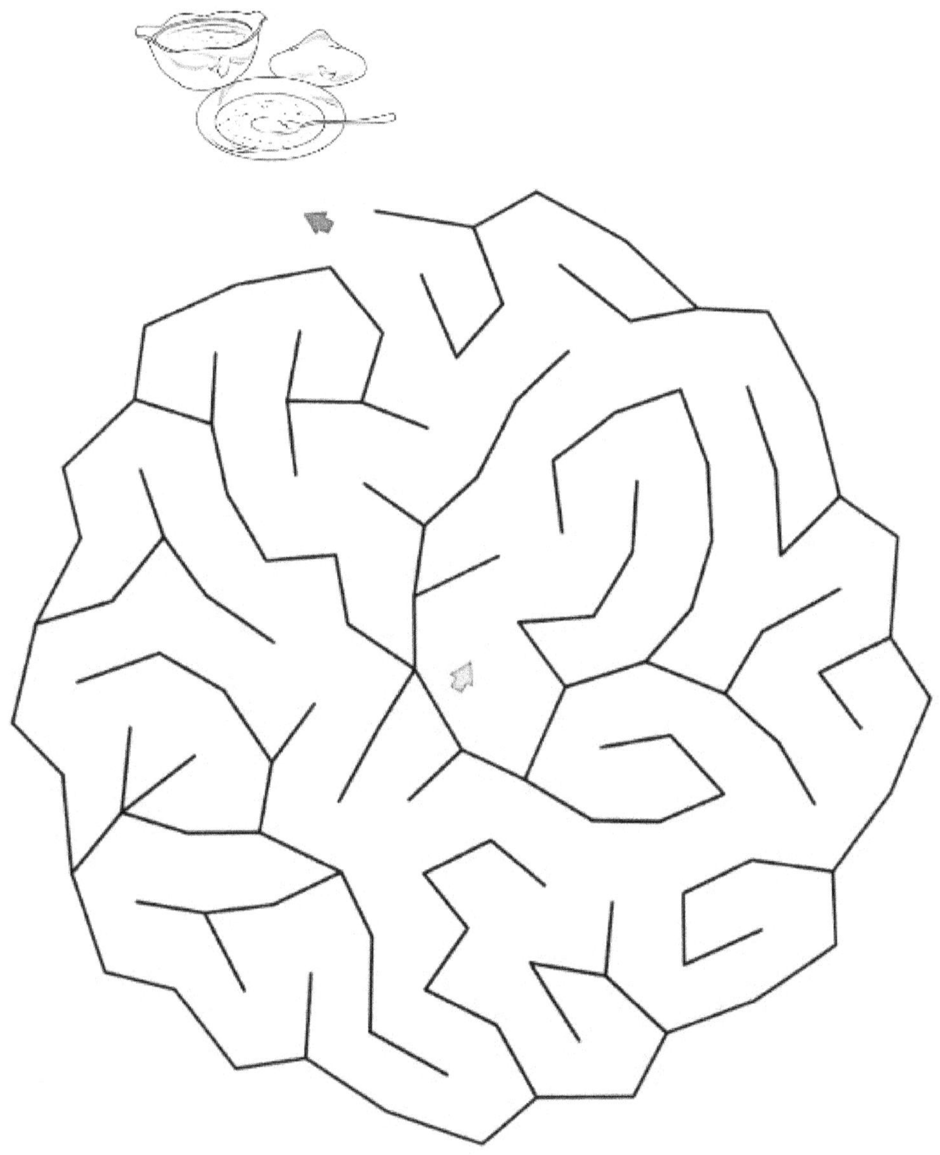

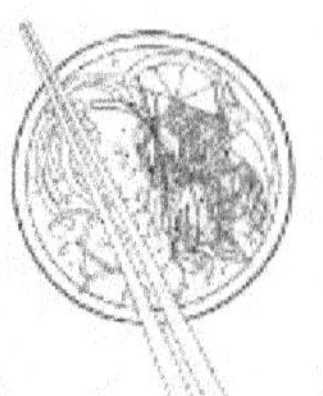

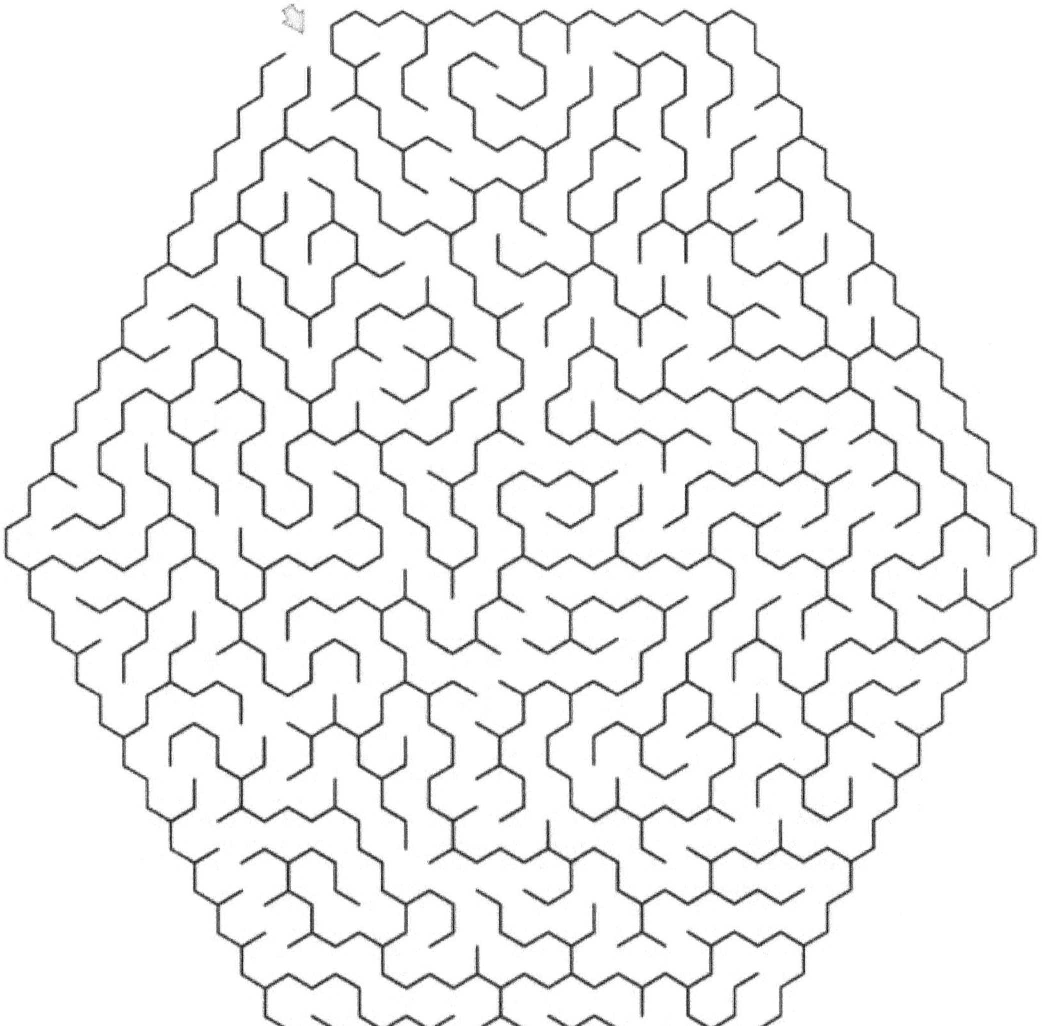

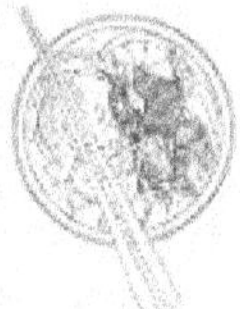

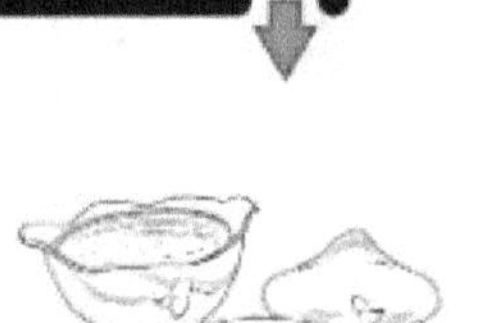

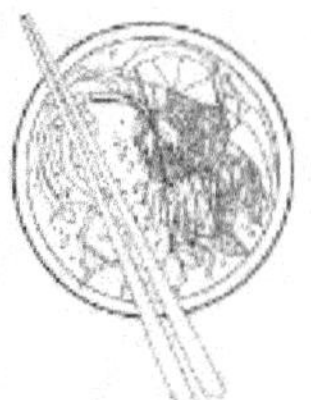

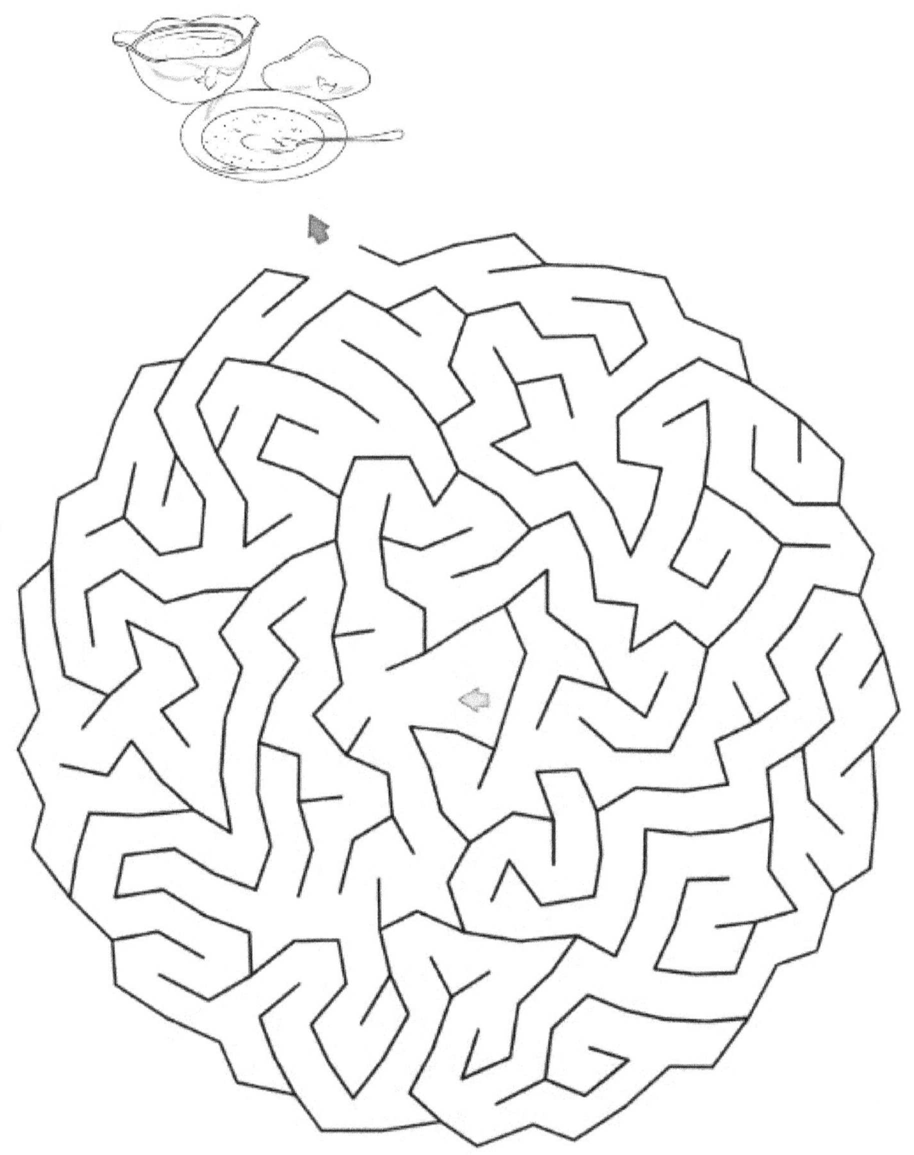

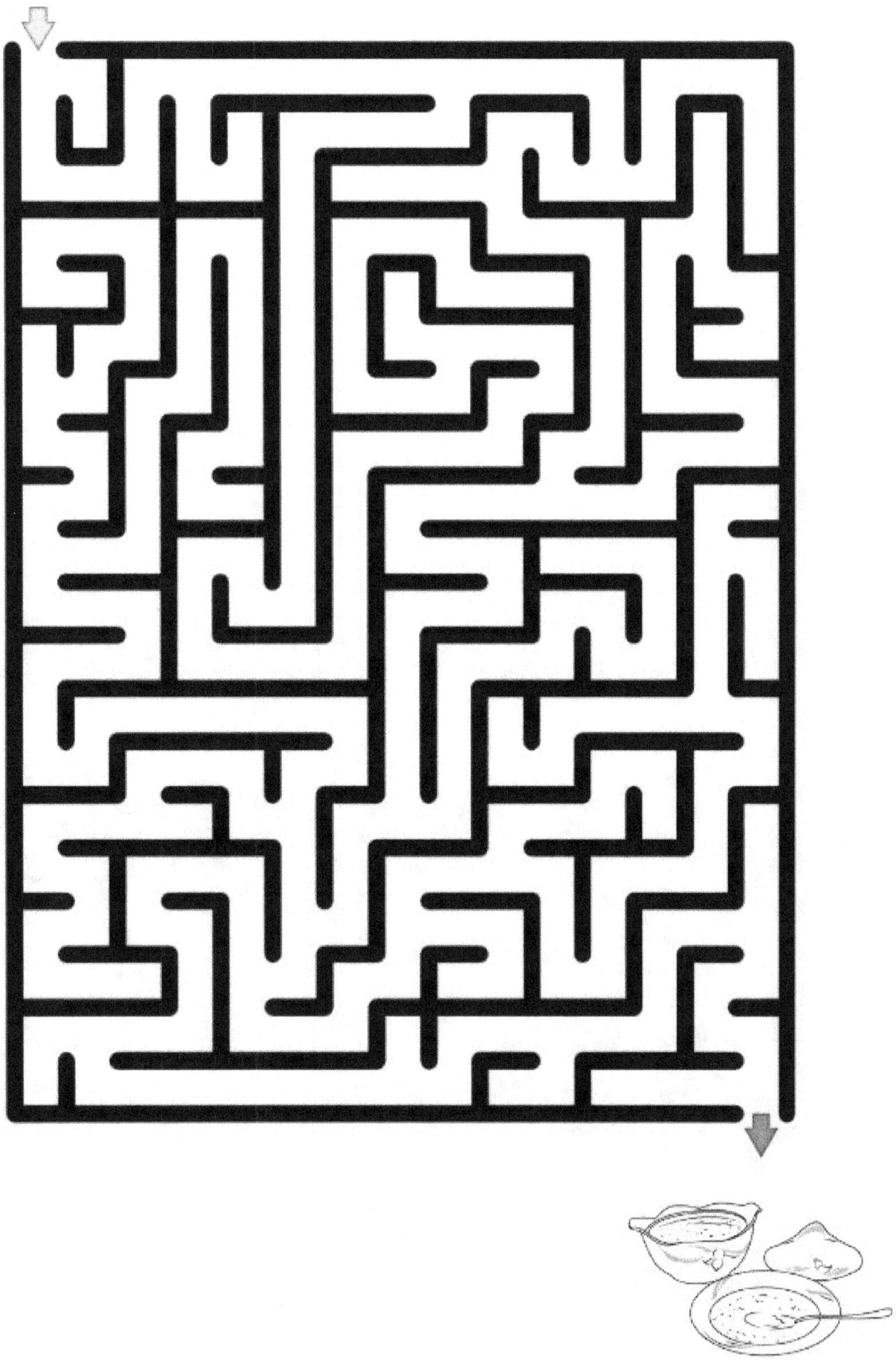

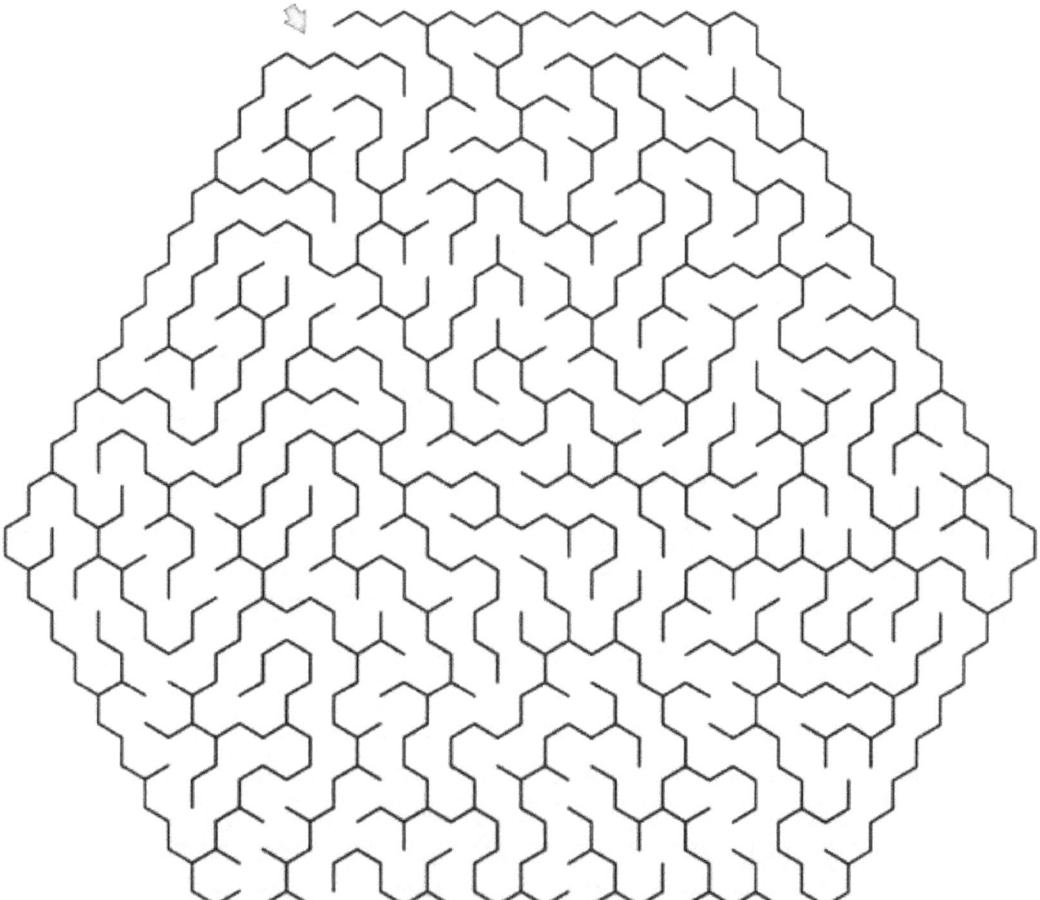

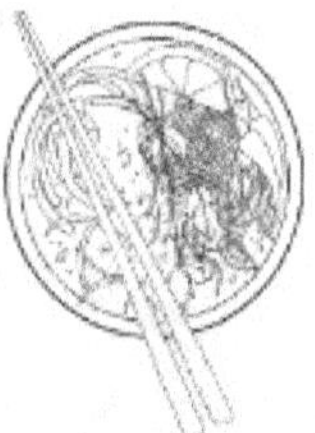